HADLEIGH
Postcard Memories

Hadleigh

Hadleigh Fire Station

Hadleigh Fire Station was opened on 2nd October 1931, the very first civic building commissioned by the burgeoning Benfleet Urban District Council (formed from the old parish councils). This much-loved building with its iconic (but temperamental) clock, still stands sentinel at the western gateway to the Town Centre, on the island site created by the 1924 bypass.

On Wednesday 28th October 2009 the Fire Brigade bid farewell to Hadleigh and relocated to Rayleigh Weir. Following a public campaign to save it, the old Fire Station was purchased by Essex County Council from Essex Fire Authority (with a Homes & Communities grant) in order that it might be used for Legacy work surrounding the 2012 Olympics. The building was extensively refurbished and leased to ACAVA (Association for Cultural Advancement through Visual Art) as artist studio spaces and as a community hall facility.

The Hadleigh & Thundersley Community Archive Group were the very first tenants, renting an office on the ground floor (with first-year funding from the now defunct Museums, Libraries and Archives Council) and on 17th September 2011 the 'Appliance Bay' thronged with visitors to the Archive's Official Launch and inaugural Local History Fair.

HADLEIGH
Postcard Memories

Robert Nichols

The Hadleigh & Thundersley
COMMUNITY ARCHIVE

DEDICATION

*To my wife Vera and
daughters, Marion and Vera*

First published in 2013 by
Hadleigh & Thundersley Community Archive
Hadleigh Old Fire Station
Hadleigh, Benfleet
Essex SS7 2PA

E-mail: hadleighhistory@gmail.com
www.hadleighhistory.org.uk

LOTTERY FUNDED

ISBN 978-0-9575958-1-1

British Library Cataloguing in Publication Data
A catalogue record for this book is available from the British Library

Production / Design: Graham Cook and David Hurrell
Colour Origination: Dot Gradations, Wickford, Essex

Printed in Spain

CONTENTS

INTRODUCTION

This is the first publishing venture of our Hadleigh & Thundersley Community Archive.

We run one of six on-line archives formed early in 2010 as a joint initiative of Debbie Peers of Essex Record Office and Sue Hampson of Essex Libraries, with the financial support of the Heritage Lottery Fund. Currently, the six archive websites get about 10,000 hits a month.

The development of the Hadleigh & Thundersley Community Archive has included public presentations at Hadleigh Library, drop-in sessions, participation in local events, hosting Hadleigh History Fair and developing a presence at Hadleigh Old Fire Station – Hadleigh's new community hub. We have also helped build a mobile phone web app, see: www.teamhadleigh.org.uk.

We are delighted to say that local residents have shown unfailing support for our archive, both by coming to organised events and contributing their personal histories to our website, as evidenced at: www.hadleighhistory.org.uk.

Perhaps stimulated by the apparently casual and relentless destruction of old properties and historic assets in our corner of south-east Essex, residents are realising the importance of documenting Hadleigh and Thundersley's constantly changing landscape. With their help, we are making previously unseen historic documents, pictures and postcards, accessible to present and future generations by publishing them on our website.

In the case of Mr Nichols, however, we instinctively felt that his unique collection of postcards and personal commentary would be best showcased in a book. We are delighted to say that funds secured from the Heritage Lottery Fund 'All Our Stories' programme have enabled us to present this, our first publication.

Happy browsing!

The Editorial Board
Hadleigh & Thundersley Community Archive

heritage lottery fund
LOTTERY FUNDED

FOREWORD

The intention of this book is to provide a visual indication of the changes that have taken place in Hadleigh since the birth of the picture postcard era – *circa* 1900 – to more or less up to World War 2, reflecting the aspects familiar to the memories of the inhabitants of that era.

The presentation of the postcards starts with views of Hadleigh's centre, the Church of St James the Less and Hadleigh Corner (so called because of London Road's large bend into, or from, the old High Street). Each route emanating from this corner is illustrated in turn.

This compilation of postcards is selected from a much larger collection that was intended to preserve impressions of the bygone parts of Essex for future generations.

As postcard production started only *circa* 1890 and topographical photographs a little later, it is not possible to go further back in time than this date. Also because many of those survivals are undated, initially only the address being permitted on the reverse, and even those which were posted and the post date legible, this date may not necessarily be a true indication of the date of the scene depicted. Therefore precise chronological order cannot always be achieved, so if errors have occurred it is hoped that they are only minor in character.

Within these limitations, it is hoped that this presentation will evoke pleasant nostalgia for the older viewer and interest and enlightenment for the younger reader who will be able to visualise the changes that have occurred during the passage of time.

Of course there may be a more comprehensive collection than mine or even some rare postcards hidden away that may come to light, that would enhance this collection. Therefore this book represents my long and arduous search for postcards that represent the area historically and hopefully will induce in others some of the pleasure that the collection has afforded me.

Robert Nichols 2013

Section 1.
The old London Road (A13) through Hadleigh High Street

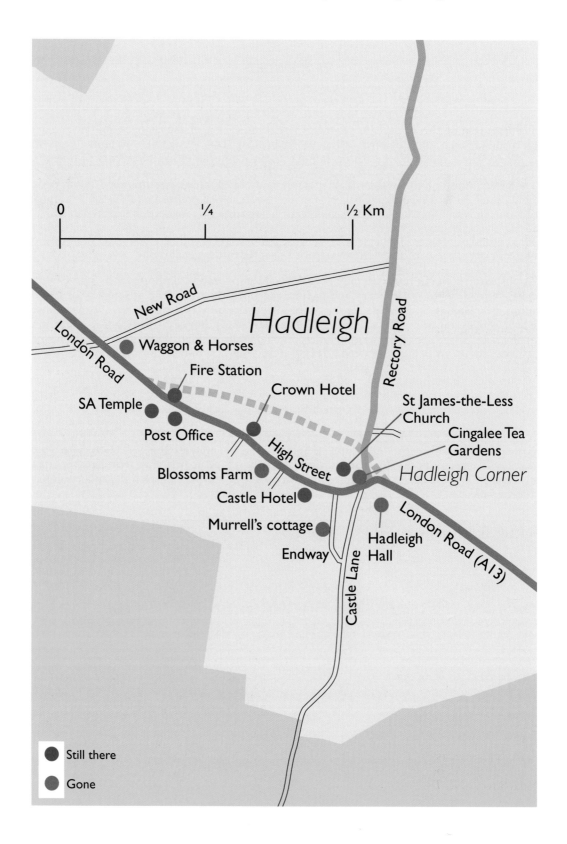

1 Hadleigh Church from the north-west
Central to the village of Hadlea (amongst other earlier names) was the church of St James the Less, built *circa* 1140, perhaps as much for a fortification as for religious purposes. This card *circa* 1902 suggests a rather small local population.
Ed. There is a school of thought that this was a Saxon church, enlarged by the Normans.

2 Hadleigh Church from the north-east
A wintry scene, as no foliage is to be seen, does reveal to the west the cottages in the old High Street and, behind the apse, those at the corner where the London Road enters the High Street. *Ed. The four nearby gravestones are extant, dated 1893, ?, 1890, 1885.*

St. James the Less Church, Hadleigh.

Observe the Apse.

The „IXL" Series.

Feby 23rd 1904.

3 Hadleigh Church, the Norman apse
This card (printed in Germany) whilst not addressed, tends to suggest that some visitors are arriving in the area, and also that the south side of the churchyard is preferred for burials.

HADLEIGH CHURCH

4 Hadleigh Church, from the east
By 1906, this card confirms that considerably more care is being taken of the church surrounds, the new chestnut fencing making a convenient perch for the three youths.
Ed. Photograph by Roberts of Hadleigh. The writer makes reference to his enjoyment of cycling, running and football, claiming that Hadleigh has a 'good village football side'.

5 Hadleigh Church, main entrance (south)
This view is of the main entrance to the church from the High Street. The approach walls are showing their age. The weather-boarded cottage is clearly occupied and has one of those indispensable and (for those days) ubiquitous tin baths outside.

6 Hadleigh Church, between 1902 and 1911
This card was written on January 4th 1912 by 'June' in Southend-on-Sea and sent to her friend 'Edie' in Westcliff-on-Sea reminding her of an appointment. The photograph however, is likely to have been from earlier. *Ed. Reverse reproduced on the inside back cover.*

7 Hadleigh Church interior
This and the next card show the conversion from oil to gas lighting, which must have occurred after 1912, as the reredos and altar were installed in that year.

8 Hadleigh Church, Easter decorations
The ornately carved reredos, which Reverend Douglas Adamson presented to the church, was a remarkable piece of work and is seen here *circa* 1930 at Easter-tide. Note the gas-lights.
Ed. Hymns Ancient & Modern, number 131, 'Christ the Lord is risen today'

DawesHeath Corner Hadleigh.

9 Hadleigh Corner, looking towards the church (Postmarked 1908)

By 1908 it seems that Hadleigh Corner (being the junction of the London Road, with roads to Daws Heath and the Castle) is requiring some traffic regulation, hence the triangle. Part of the church is visible behind the cyclist, the remainder obscured by trees. The route to the Castle is not sign-posted.

Hadleigh.

10 Hadleigh Corner, looking up Rectory Road (postmarked 1920)

Viewed from Hadleigh Corner, we see Rectory Road leading to Daws Heath and Thundersley with the Hadleigh 'Fourpennies' plying for trade. The finger-post pointing to the left, reads to Rayleigh and London and that to the right to Leigh and Southend i.e. the A13 in infancy. The cottages on the left hand side of Rectory Road still stand (beside a car park in 2013.)

11 Hadleigh Hall
These two views postmarked 1908 and 1910 clearly indicate the convenience of the
Hadleigh Corner. This one (taken from the church fence) shows the walled Hadleigh Hall.
The 'Fourpennies' are also there waiting.
Ed. Produced by Bell's Photo Co Ltd, Leigh-on-Sea

12 A Horse & Cart Parade
Here a (mock) Scotsman standing by a mounted knight (or possibly a clown) attract a
youthful audience.   *Ed. Produced by W. Sullivan, Photographer, Hadleigh. The Chelmsford
Chronical reported a horse parade and competition took place at Hadleigh on Wednesday 9th
June 1909 in aid of Victoria Hospital, Southend. Similar events took place in 1910 and 1911.*

13 Hadleigh transport

The age of mechanical transport has arrived! Yet with uniformed driver and conductor, few passenger places are available. The destination board between and just above the headlamps shows 'Leigh.' Thought to have been taken *circa* 1905.

14 Hadleigh as a tourist destination

This 'charabanc' *circa* 1920 is registered to 43 Ambleside Drive, Southend-on-Sea and the crest over the rear solid tyred-wheel reads 'Royal Sovereign' Phone 707. Possibly day trippers? The finger pointer on the notice board is to the left – to the 'Castle (something)' but the location has not been established for certain. Note the speed restriction!

15 Public Transport

By 1922 a bus service appears well established and is known as the 'Thundersley, Hadleigh and District Motors Ltd.' At least five people have gathered (in addition to the driver and conductor) and, presumably, are potential travellers. No destination board is visible, but probably Leigh or Southend. Note still solid tyres and the heavily festooned telegraph pole.

16 Hadleigh Corner from Castle lane

Dated 1923, passengers are arriving. The garage behind the bus was later replaced by a larger one built on the corner of Oak Road, and this still exists. Note the shops on the corner of the High Street and the gateway to Hadleigh Hall (and mail box) on the corner of Castle Lane on the right side of the picture.

17 Charabanc at Hadleigh Corner
By *circa* 1927 pneumatic tyres have appeared, but few other comforts. With more gentlemen than ladies (16:7) this is more likely to be a works outing than a day trippers' excursion. No paid holidays then, only a 'Beano', if you were lucky.
Ed. Rectory Road extended past the church's eastern gate.

18 Hadleigh Corner, looking north
Rectory Road is seen ahead leading to Daws Heath, with the Southend/London road in the foreground turning the corner into the High Street on the left. The bus garage is clearly seen here.

19 High Street at Hadleigh Corner
As seen in this 1911 card, J. S. Martin was a tailor and outfitter and G. E. Perkins a tobacconist and confectioner who occupied these 'High Street Corner' shops together with the embryonic Cingalee Restaurant and Tea Gardens.

20 The Cingalee Tea Gardens
The Tea Gardens faced towards Leigh on the sharp bend of Hadleigh Corner. It backs directly on to the churchyard from which it was screened by much foliage. A pot of tea with a roll and butter was 6d – that is 2$^{1}/_{2}$p in modern parlance.

21 The Cingalee Restaurant

The Cingalee Restaurant & Tea Gardens eventually occupied all these shops and dominated the corner for several years, as this 1923 card confirms. It had Tea Gardens at each end (see cards 16, 18 and 20.) Note that the posters in the window offer a 'pot of tea' with two different food options for 7d and 10d respectively.

22 This view of the staff must have been taken before the more formal waitress uniforms were adopted, as in postcard 21, but no doubt the service was entirely satisfactory.
Ed. The Cingalee was a popular 1904 musical by Lionel Monkton, about colonial tea planters in Ceylon. One of its most popular songs was entitled, 'Tea, tea, tea'. Southend Operatic and Dramatic Society were the first amateur group to ever perform it, in 1912.

23 High Street, looking west from Castle Lane junction
Rounding 'Cingalee' corner the main area of the High Street is in view, including some shops and inhabitants. The mother and clinging small daughter are close to the church entrance and almost opposite is Endway (see card 26.)

24 136-134 High Street, the old Hadleigh Hall lodge
This butchery was almost opposite the 'Tea Gardens' and its yard, with slaughterhouse at rear, bordered Castle Lane. There is plenty of beef on view and at least four rabbits, or hares. *Ed. Jonathan Webster set up his butchery business in c. 1895. He left Hadleigh during WW1. This building survives (2013) as a bathroom and kitchen showroom.*

25 Outen's High Street stores

F. Outen ran a multiple business being greengrocer, fruiterer, confectioner and tobacconist, and the large signboard by the shop door even advertises 'Castle Cafe' Restaurant and Teas. It was situated on the corner of Endway.

26 Endway

One of these cottages in Endway was the home of 'Cunning' James Murrell who had a considerable reputation in the area for his mystical and curative abilities *circa* 1810 to 1860. The lane linked the High Street (and Church) with Castle Lane and formed part of the ancient route between church and river.

27 High Street cottages by church entrance

This and the next somewhat earlier views – *circa* 1900 – confirm a considerably earlier origin of the village, note the crumbling walls and sagging roofs. Old 'Blossoms' farmhouse (with ivy on it) still remains but the farm had long gone.

28 High Street, south side from the church entrance

The middle cottage now provides both barber and tobacconist. The sign at the first door reads 'Haircutting, shaving, shampooing saloon' whilst that one at the second door (with the step) reads 'Adkin & Sons, Nut Brown tobaccos London' both being rather *Bijou* facilities. Mr Grimes is the proprietor of the fruiterer & confectioner, where the road bends.

29 The Castle Hotel before the new facade and roof

This 'coach' appears almost ready to depart with seven passengers aboard (six seated), but with the steps still down; perhaps latecomers are awaited. The lady in the 'gig' is also waiting for her driver – but they are at a hostelry after all! This card is postmarked 1908.

30 High Street at the dawn of the Twentieth Century

These passengers surely have only recently arrived? At least ten ladies, three gents (not including the driver attending the horses) and two children can be seen, with no obvious single objective. Perhaps just a gentle stroll on a warm August day *circa* 1904?

31 The Castle Hotel, High Street

A tranquil village scene – a lady with two children outside the butcher's and a 'cabbie' awaiting a fare. The road traffic sign suggests a different situation as it reads Dangerous Corner. Note the hotel's modernised façade with Hadleigh Castle on its sign-board and 'Ye Old Castle Hotel' engraved over the main door.

32 A much more active scene, with an original 'Dennis' omnibus, with a loaded top deck and several open umbrellas, for sun protection. The omnibus (locally registered) has Rayleigh as its destination and the signpost reads 'All buses to Thundersley and Rayleigh stop here'. The private car is from another area (by its registration).
Ed. The building was later extended to the right and the gable chimney moved across.

Tea Gardens, Castle Hotel, Hadleigh. 77529

33 The Castle Hotel Tea Gardens
Dated 1929, this postcard is of the Tea Gardens at the side of the Castle Hotel –
convenient for the bus stop – now the inn's car park. Note the teapots – no teabags in those
days and personal service not 'Get it yourself'.
Ed. This is now the pub car park (2013). The building was later extended at this gable end.

Hadleigh. 77617.

34 High Street, from nearby Endway
Here in the shadow is another grocer's (on the corner of Endway) with a recently delivered
stack of boxes in the doorway – (including four of Nestlés Milk). Note the vehicles of
WWI vintage near Lily Smith's general store.
Ed. Mary Pickford's 1922 film, Tess of the Storm Country, is advertised on the hoarding.

35 High Street, looking west

This card, dated 1908, reveals that a compact row of purpose-built shops (as opposed to converted cottages) known as The Parade had been built *circa* 1900, in order to cater for the surge in population largely caused by the Salvation Army's arrival in the 1890s with their Farm Colony and brickworks.

36 The Parade, High Street

This is a reverse view of similar date. The first shop is Schofield & Martin's grocery, agents for W. & A. Gilbey wine and spirits merchant (famous for their gin). Besides Trumans and Whitbread's beers and stout, Pratts and Shell Motor Spirit is also 'Sold here' (in cans apparently – as no pumps are visible).   *Ed. Telegraph poles and trees have been 'cropped'.*

37 High Street, looking west

The appearance of the new Fire Station (the tall building in the distance) dates this view to post 1931. Lily Smith is still trading (until 1933) in the corner shop and 'Smith Bro' are trading as butchers, but Homestead Road and a new shop, Emmerton Dairies, appears where 'Blossoms' used to be.

38 Times are already changing: both the Smiths' businesses have gone and the corner shop is now an electrician's, charging wireless accumulators (lead-acid batteries). The placard on the left is advertising Robert Montgomery in 'Live, Love and Learn' (1937) at the huge, new Ritz cinema, situated at the top of Pier Hill (gone since 1981 and replaced by The Royals). *Ed. The new George VI pillar box nowadays resides on the opposite side, by Homestead Way.*

39 Arthur Yeaxlee, the draper, occupied the first shop in the Parade (later it became the Post Office) but, as seen previously, there was also at one time a chemist (Perkins), a bakery (Polley; Reynolds; Dossetts), a tea shop, a grocer and a general store (Schofield & Martin). The Corona Cinema (Leigh) poster (at the Castle gatepost) states the feature film as Tom Walls in 'The Blarney Stone'(released 1933) and the supporting one 'Oliver Twist'.

40 **High Street, in 1934 (or before)**
To the fore is Alfred Charles Lawrence's tea, confectionery and tobacco shop. One placard for the Daily Express reads 'Queen Victoria's letters, Reflections', the placard for the Herald reads 'Gov't moves against Profiteers'. Later, Lawrence's two daughters took on the business.

41 The Crown Hotel, High Street

There is no mistaking the name of this hotel (better seen in card 42) with 'The Crown Hotel' engraved over the main door and also painted on the Dutch-style gable. The card is dated 1905, but the building dates back to *circa* 1769. Note the bare trees and the children in warm wear.

42 The Crown Hotel, Castle Hotel and Blossoms Farmhouse

This photograph indicates the relative position of the hotel in the High Street and must have been taken mid-1920s as the farmhouse is still seen, extreme right. Below the window sills, the hotel walls look to be in poor condition, but note that the cyclists saw no need to security chain their mounts, in those days.

43 Balchin's Bakery, High Street

Adjacent to the Crown premises was a row of cottages, the second of which was a cottage bakery, operated by a succession of owners. Walter Balchin is named here but others also included Heathcote and Batchelor.
Ed. Hadleigh Library was built on this site.

44 High Street, postmarked 1920 (but probably pre WW1)

Most intriguing is 'Schneider and Coare' as proprietors of the bakery. Across the road are more shops: another hairdresser (H. A. Wallis)and a confectioner. The plot beyond these shops became the site of Tom Reynold's scrap-metal yard (and now Homestead Court).
Ed. Otto Herman Schneider appears in the 1911 Census and the 1912 Directory for Hadleigh.

HADLEIGH POST OFFICE

45 Hadleigh Post Office, High Street

The Post Office (so nominated between the first floor windows) is a department of E. Potter's General Drapers and Stationery establishment. It was situated (rather remotely) near to the west-end of the High Street. Note the ladies' bicycles. The view is dated by postmark as 1906. *Ed. Nowadays this building is the Conservative Club, number 24.*

46 Stannard's Stores, High Street

This is a nearer view of the middle building seen in the previous card. It is of Charles Richard Stannard's grocery and provisions store and is dated 1907. The assistant on the step-ladder appears to be about to straighten the poster.
Ed. Nowadays (2013) this same building (nos. 4–6) is a Bathroom and Kitchen Showroom.

47 Jackaman's Stores, High Street
Later, the same building is Jackaman's Stores advertising boots, shoes and hardware with window-stickers for methylated spirit, turpentine and linseed oil, but what the 'Monsters' are (over on the left and also on postcard 44) cannot be determined.
Ed. Jackaman's appears in Hadleigh Directories for 1910/12/14 but gone by 1917.

48 High Street from London Road
The 'Y' junction is apparent here. The Salvation Army had the Young People's Hall and Temple built in 1938 (by L. Upson & Sons). It suffered some bomb damage in 1940. Their brickworks are advertising 'Good Bricks' at 'Reasonable Prices' on the board behind the Austin Seven.   *Ed. Temple replaced in 2003. Weather-boarded house extant 2013.*

High Street, Hadleigh.

148807

49 The Fire Station (see frontispiece)

The High Street reconverges with London Road and the by-pass just around this bend (see cards 48 and 50). The junction is dominated by the Fire Station (built 1931) seen on the right side.

Ed. Circa 1941. Harold House in the distance. Note telephone kiosk outside Fire Station.

HADLEIGH. 41160

50 London Road, looking west towards Victoria House Corner

Around the bend of the High Street, the London Road continues on its way *circa* 1913. The Waggon and Horses pub is the last building on the right next to the smithy/wheelwright with three waggons outside. On the left the large billboard proclaims 'The Salvation Army Land and Industrial Colony and Poultry Farm'. *Ed. This road is now dual carriageway.*

Section 2.
The London Road by-pass (constructed in 1924), also known as New Road or Kingsway

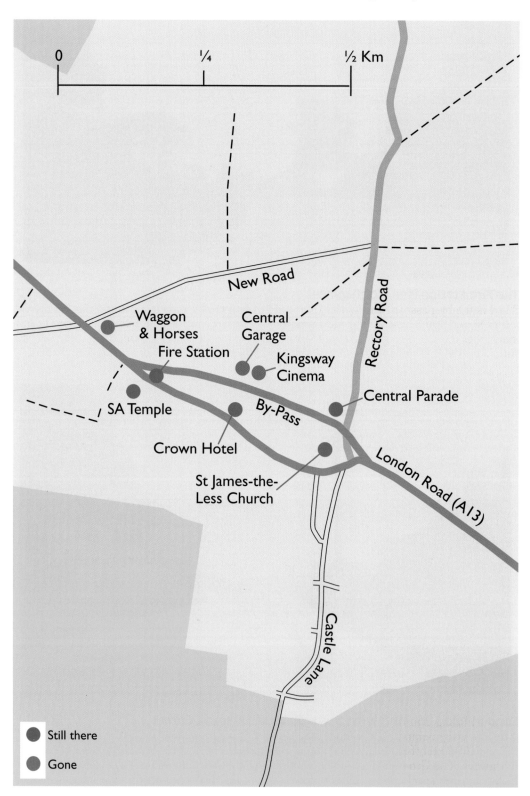

New Road

Rectory Road

Waggon & Horses

Central Garage

Fire Station

Kingsway Cinema

Central Parade

SA Temple

By-Pass

Crown Hotel

St James-the-Less Church

London Road (A13)

Castle Lane

Still there

Gone

Hadleigh, showing Church

51 Hadleigh by-pass, looking towards the town centre

Here is the by-pass constructed in 1924 to relieve potential dangers in and approaching the High Street, and to absorb the increasing traffic that the nucleus of a central shopping area had formed. The large hoarding is Gordon Wilson's with land and bungalows for sale, the smaller for Arthur Yeaxlee.

New Road, Hadleigh

52 More building is in progress here. The bus, a No 3, is destined for Benfleet. Two motorcycles are appearing behind it. The land/bungalow sale hoarding now reads W. Bruce Peart F.A.C. of 508/10 Westcliff-on-Sea. Note that the lady with the pram prefers the road to the shingle pathways. The Crown Hotel is also indicated by the sign board extreme left.

Ed. Note the clear view from the Crown through to Church and Rectory Road!

53 Looking west towards the Kingsway Cinema

Ribbon shop development continues, Mr Sharp the optician had the first one; another is the Broadway Bakery; the clock features the name 'Toyland' and the last is Arthur Yeaxlee's new larger store. This card is dated 1941, but the Kingsway Cinema was built in 1936. The Central Garage ends the line.

54 The Kingsway Shops

This photograph was clearly taken from the roof of the cinema and gives a fine view of the Kingsway shopping parade giving this name to the by-pass. Many tombstones are visible, and on the bend is a large estate agency and Barclays Bank. Between the trees the road can be seen continuing to Southend.

Central Parade, Hadleigh, Essex.

55 Central Parade looking west

The entry to the by-pass (Central Parade/Kingsway/London Road, whichever) in this busy view includes the LCS (London Co-operative Society) haberdashery (previously Keddie's), the Dinky Café, Chalk's greengrocery, chemist, LCS butcher & grocer and Howard's Dairies.

68829. HIGH ROAD HADLEIGH.

56 London Road, north side towards the Waggon & Horses

Looking again at the London Road continuation, an extra house has been added, that of Mr D. Stibbards of the local undertaking family business (3rd generation still trading). All now gone for a supermarket car park. The Waggon & Horses stands proud on the end but even this has now surrendered to a block of apartments.

Section 3.
Chapel Lane and New Road off the London Road by the War Memorial

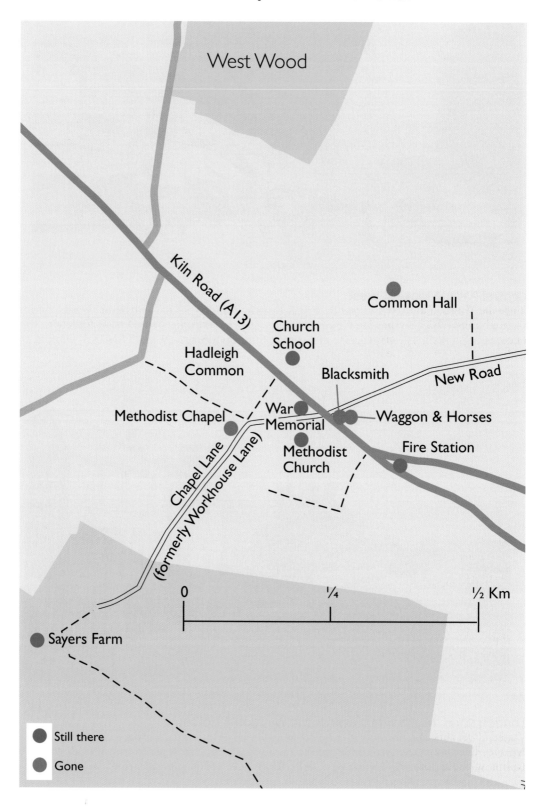

West Wood

Kiln Road (A13)

Common Hall

Church School

Hadleigh Common

Blacksmith

New Road

Methodist Chapel

War Memorial

Waggon & Horses

Chapel Lane (formerly Workhouse Lane)

Methodist Church

Fire Station

0   ¼   ½ Km

Sayers Farm

Still there

Gone

RECREATION GROUND AND WAR MEMORIAL, HADLEIGH. 3216.

57 Hadleigh War Memorial

Here the Waggon and Horses (with that name blazoned across the frontage) is seen through the WWI Memorial Gardens (which were dedicated in 1922). An alehouse has occupied this site since prior 1841. The board on the side wall shows Henry Luker & Co Ltd as the owners, whose brewery was in Southend High Street.

The Blacksmith's Hadleigh.

58 Blacksmith's Shop, by the Waggon & Horses

Dated 1906, this card is of the smithy, a glimpse of which is seen in card 57 through the foliage. The three youths are standing in the entrance to New Road, which runs obliquely to link with Rectory Road/Daws Heath Road. Commonhall Lane also joins at this point.

59 London Road from junction with Chapel Lane, looking west
Circa 1920 a different viewpoint (from that of the previous card) reveals that it is actually of a crossroads, with Chapel Lane (earlier known as Workhouse Lane for the obvious reason) which also led to Sayers Farm belonging to the Salvation Army. The trees in the distance are close to the western boundary of the Hadleigh Parish.

60 Hadleigh National School *circa* 1910
Here is the first dedicated school in Hadleigh, built in 1855 and extended (at the front) in 1895. It was built on a plot approximately in line with the head of the cyclist standing in London Road, in card 59.
Ed. The building remains in 2013 as Sandcastles nursery school.

61 London Road, looking east

Postmarked 1909, this view was taken from close to the Church School as that building shown in the last card was later known. The middle telegraph pole is near Chapel Lane and, opposite, is New Road. In the distance are houses in the High Street.
Ed. Produced by Bells Photo Co Ltd of Westcliff-on-Sea.

62 Chapel Lane (formerly Workhouse Lane), looking north

Here we are looking up Chapel Lane towards the London Road. In the far distance is the old Church School. The house on the left is Killarney and the one beyond, through the trees, is Holboro House (still standing 2013).
Ed. Holboro House was built for Alfred Hawks, village schoolmaster for 43 years.

63 Chapel Lane, the old chapel and the recreation ground

Dated 1925, the original Methodist Chapel, (built 1865) is seen, but it was superseded by a much larger one, closer to the London Road. A Mr J. Attwood had this chapel next, for his photographic studio. The recreation ground, the allotments and the war memorial garden were all part of the old Hadleigh Common.

64 Chapel Lane, looking south-west

The view of this card postmarked 4th August 1914, can be positioned with reference to the poplar tree and lamp-post in the previous card. The adult and three children (one girl and two boys) are clearly posing for the camera.

65 New Road, looking east

At the cross-roads, as previously explained, is New Road opposite Chapel Lane and this view, postmarked 1913, has been taken from the London Road end because, initially, most of the buildings were on the south side of the road.

Ed. The first "semi" on the right is now numbered 54 and 56.

66 New Road, looking east

The writer of this card, postmarked 1922, confirms the review of card 65, as he actually refers to the entrance to Templewood Road, which is near the lamp post on the left.

Ed. Many of these dwellings still exist: 2nd from right is now 78 and 80 and next is 86. This postcard is published by Padgett's of Leigh-on-Sea.

Section 4.
Rayleigh Road & Benfleet Road from Victoria House Corner

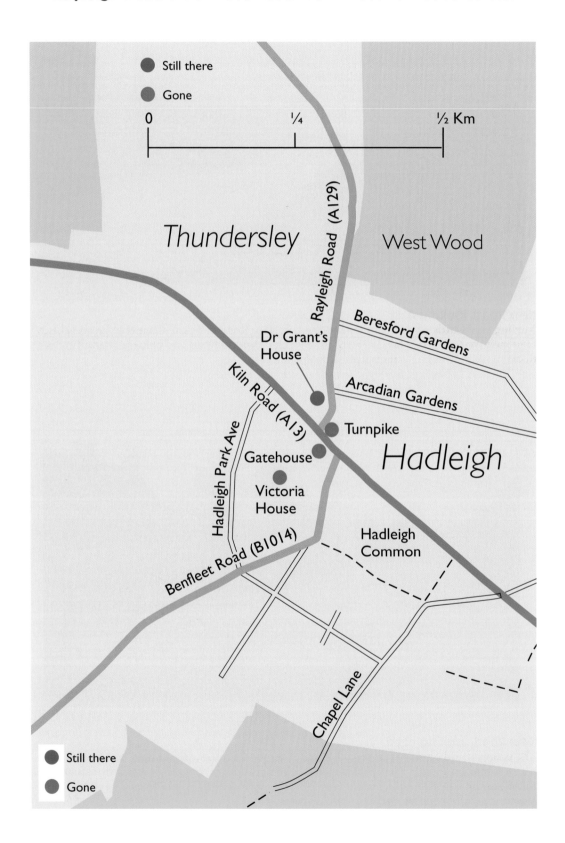

THE CROSS ROADS, HADLEIGH.

67 Victoria House Corner and the gatehouse

Moving westwards from the Chapel Lane/New Road cross-roads, the next junction, at the Hadleigh western boundary, looked like this in 1906. Kiln Road continues ahead, Rayleigh Road to the right and Benfleet and Canvey to the left.

VICTORIA HOUSE

68 Victoria House

The gateway and gate-house in card 67 dominated the entrance to the (20 acre) estate of Victoria House, formerly Hadleigh House, which was owned by some illustrious persons, as well as the Salvation Army. Whilst now long gone, its memory lives on in that the junction is still known as Victoria House Corner. *Ed. This card is franked June 1906.*

Cross Roads, Hadleigh

69 Victoria House Corner, looking west

By the 1920s the Victoria House estate is already being whittled away, first on the periphery, by shops appearing then, when the house was finally demolished, (sometime before World War 2) the whole estate was finally consumed by houses, including Hadleigh Park Avenue and Pinetrees. *Ed. Ramuz auctioned off the Hadleigh Park Estate in 136 lots in August 1923.*

VICTORIA CORNER HADLEIGH

70 Victoria House Corner

Whether open-top buses can be considered as progress, except in capacity, is a moot point but they operated well into the 1930s. Also traders now have vans (Fords perhaps?). Note that the gate house still remains and that the grocer W. Cook & Co has commandeered the name 'Victoria House' for his shop.

71 Hadleigh Turnpike Cottage

This is the old turnpike cottage, though long past performing its original purpose of collecting tolls from the traffic. It was situated at the corner of Rayleigh Road and London Road and is here viewed from Benfleet Road.

72 Dr Grant's House, Rayleigh Road

This is the entrance to Rayleigh Road from the London Road and is dated 1906. The two workmen appear to be trimming the undergrowth by the hedges of the woods of which only West Wood (at the bottom of the hill) remains. The house still stands and was the home of Dr Grant whose exuberant moustache fascinated me when I was a child.

Rayleigh Road, Hadleigh.

112554

73 Rayleigh Road, junction with Kiln Road

This is Rayleigh Road in 1934 with houses on both sides and even up close to the corner. The person visible on the pathway is on the corner of Arcadian Gardens and the large hoarding in that road is advertising houses for sale in the Falbro Garden 'Suburb' Estate for £750! The distant signpost indicates Beresford Gardens.

Victoria House Corner, Hadleigh.

74 Victoria House Corner, looking west

Shops and facilities have now progressed into the Benfleet Road. Next to the grocer's is an ice cream and tea cabin, then a ginger beer and ices garden with the name-board reading the Victoria Kum Bak Courts and, finally, a coal depot, house removals and estate agency run by Mr John P. Seligsohn. The signpost also points to the Arterial Road i.e. the A127.

CROSS ROADS, HADLEIGH   650.

75 Dr Grant's and Turnpike Cottage

The majority of the surface area in this view is now covered by a large traffic roundabout controlling the four roads. It is gardened, with a central clock standard dedicated to a local parliamentarian (Sir Bernard Braine) and, in 2012, the statue of a cyclist has been added to commemorate the Olympic Mountain Bike races held locally.

Benfleet Road, Hadleigh.

76 Venture Stores, Benfleet Road, looking south

Shops are now spreading along the Benfleet Road from Victoria Corner. The first is the Venture Stores of P. Hallett which appears to be a second-hand shop with a dress-maker's dummy and pieces of furniture outside and maybe the motorcycle combination also for sale. The road bends to the right and part of the Lynton Estate can be seen ahead.

77 Benfleet Road, looking north

The sunblind next to the second-hand shop in the previous card states 'newsagent & library'. The next new row contains a tea shop, the W. L. Robertson's confectioner and tobacconist, next a grocer's and, finally, a hardware shop (presumably) as only 'Oil Dealers' can be read for identification.

78 Benfleet Road, St John's Road junction

This view *circa* 1913 was Benfleet Road around the bend at the Lynton Estate (opposite Hadleigh Park Avenue). Leading to South Benfleet and Canvey, Benfleet Road is now lined with exclusive properties. The house in front (No. 69) is on the corner of an unmade St John's Road. The roofs of a few other houses can just be seen between the trees.

Section 5.
Rectory Road into Daws Heath and into Thundersley

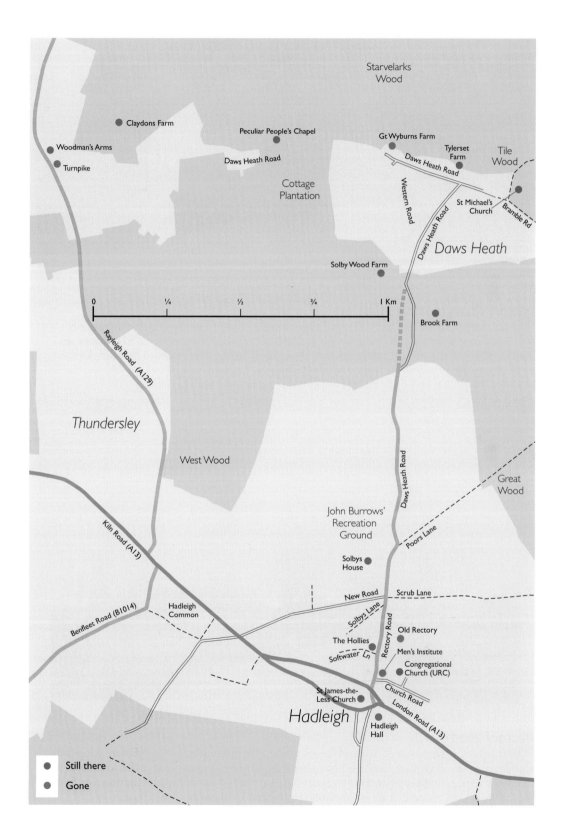

Starvelarks Wood

Claydons Farm

Peculiar People's Chapel

Woodman's Arms

Turnpike

Daws Heath Road

Cottage Plantation

Gt Wyburns Farm

Tylerset Farm

Tile Wood

Daws Heath Road

Western Road

Daws Heath Road

St Michael's Church

Bramble Rd

Daws Heath

Solby Wood Farm

0   ¼   ½   ¾   1 Km

Brook Farm

Rayleigh Road (A129)

Thundersley

West Wood

Daws Heath Road

Great Wood

John Burrows' Recreation Ground

Poors Lane

Kiln Road (A13)

Solbys House

New Road

Scrub Lane

Benfleet Road (B1014)

Hadleigh Common

Solbys Lane

Rectory Road

Old Rectory

The Hollies

Men's Institute

Softwater Ln

Congregational Church (URC)

St James-the-Less Church

Church Road

Hadleigh

London Road (A13)

Hadleigh Hall

● Still there
● Gone

51

Hadleigh Corner.

79 Rectory Road, looking south

Having now glimpsed an early view of the westerly route from Hadleigh Corner, a
northerly one next (first introduced via card 10). This next view is from Rectory Road
itself looking south *circa* 1910 (though postmarked 1922). The roofs of buildings in the
High Street are just visible.

HADLEIGH

80 Rectory Road

Whilst very similar to card 79, this one was taken further back, as the boy on the left is
standing on the corner of Church Road. Because of the perspective it is difficult to
pinpoint where the by-pass will eventually be, but it must be in the area of the two trees in
the centre of the picture. The notice board is for the Congregational Church.

81 Rectory Road, Church Road junction

Still a very rural aspect to Rectory Road *circa* 1911 the only (brick) dwellings apart from the hidden rectory being this group. The nearer one is the Congregational church manse. The little girl is standing on the corner of an unmade Church Road.

Ed. This photo appears contemporary with the previous one and card 83.

82 Hadleigh Men's Institute

This card, written in 1920, depicts the Men's Institute in Rectory Road, previously the Congregational Church manse. This group of buildings has now succumbed to a large clothes store and other shops, opposite to which is now a car park and toilet block. The latter stands over a large natural pond where I clearly remember having caught newts *circa*1930.

83 Rectory Road, looking south

The two weatherboard cottages seen (also in card No 10) still exist and are easily recognisable. In the distance, several horse-taxis ('Hadleigh Fourpennies' – 4d being the fare to Leigh) line the wall of Hadleigh Hall, the roof of which appears behind the flag pole. *Ed. The reverse of this card, post-marked 7pm 23 Dec 1919, is reproduced on the title page.*

84 Rectory Road, looking towards Daws Heath

By *circa* 1927 more building has occurred. The fence on the left is that of the cottages in card 83, which are on the corner of Softwater Lane. The large house in the lane (above fence) is The Hollies, home of Edgar Munday, Councillor (unpaid), well known for his activities for Hadleigh's benefit.   *Ed. This house (altered) is now a doctors' surgery.*

85 The Rectory

This was the old Rectory built 1856 and situated in generous grounds, approximately behind where the first three people are in card 84. It has now been replaced by a more modern building and much of the grounds have become Rectory Close with more dwellings.

Rectory Road, Hadleigh.   138224

86 Rectory Road, towards Solbys Corner

By the 1930s there was little land available for extra buildings. New Road is marked here by the street lamp on the left (past the second telegraph pole) and Scrub Lane directly opposite. Ahead, round Solbys Corner, begins Daws Heath Road and, to the right, Poors Lane. These houses remain extant in 2013.

87 Rectory Road, eastern side beyond Scrub Lane
Circa 1930 this double-fronted nearly-new house situated between Scrub Lane and the corner shown next (card 88) is being offered for sale: eight rooms, two WCs, a bath, grounds 100 ft x 200 ft, plus a well! Price £650 or rent £35 per annum. It remains still, with little alteration apparent.

88 The baker's cart at Solbys
Dated 1913 this corner is that seen at the far end of the road in card 86. The wall is the corner boundary of Solbys occupied by Alderman J. H. Burrows. Following his death the land was bequeathed for recreation and known by his name. Rectory Road continues northwards as Daws Heath Road.

89 Looking north along Western Road and Daws Heath Road

A short excursion northwards along Daws Heath Road brings us to this junction. Daws Heath Road continues to the right, but shortly turns left and continues westwards until being joined again by Western Road, which is the left-hand fork seen in this view *circa* 1956. We are now in the parish of Thundersley.

90 Pond in Daws Heath

This obviously useful pond (not only for two water-fowl) was located in the bend where Western Road rejoins Daws Heath Road. It is now built over. Note the antiquated way of spelling 'Dawes' Heath.

91 Great Wyburns Farm and pond
This view, not dated but presumed *circa* 1930s, is from across the pond seen in the previous card (No. 90), with a good sight of Great Wyburns Farm, just facing Western Road.

92 The Triangle near Great Wyburns
Here is the actual junction of Western Road curving westward into Daws Heath Road. The finger post to the left points to Rayleigh and Thundersley, that to the right Bramble Hall, a large house sited ¾ mile away, east down Bramble Road.

93 Daws Heath Road, looking east from near Great Wyburns

This and the next card show aspects of the east/west section of the Daws Heath Road. This view (taken from close to the more northerly Western Road junction) is looking eastwards, to where the Bramble Hall finger-post is just visible. The little shop is advertising Empire Lamp Oil, gas and oil lamps being the common means of illumination in those days.

94 Daws Heath Road, looking east from near Hillside Cottage

Still looking to the east, but from much further west, the view is delightfully rural. The white (wooden) building in the distance (partially hidden by the brick built house) was the Peculiar People's Chapel (a significant religious sect in Essex at the time) but now a private residence. Hillside Cottage, on the right, is Grade 2-listed.

95 The Woodmans Arms, Thundersley
Here Daws Heath Road meets Rayleigh Road (looking towards Victoria House Corner). The public house is the Woodman's Arms (which still exists) with the old toll house across the road. For interest, this card is written by a father to his daughter Catherine in New York, USA and dated 1912, the year when RMS Titanic sank.

96 Toll House, Thundersley
An earlier view *circa* 1900 of the same junction showing Rayleigh Road in poor condition (pot holes and puddles). The finger-post pointing right (to Hart Road) reads Bowers (Gifford) Pitsea and London.

Rectory Road, Hadleigh

97 Looking north from the Church, up Rectory Road

We return to Hadleigh with two pre-WWII cards and with Keddie's the drapers occupying this shop on the corner of the by-pass and Rectory Road. Other shops are spreading along the road. The distant roof visible is that of the cottages in card 83.

Corner Rectory Road, Hadleigh.

98 Central Parade and Rectory Road businesses

This view of the corner presents a busier scene, with Norton's (a removal firm), Ruggins' confectionery, Barclays Bank, and E & S Garage selling Power petrol at 1s/4d (7p) a gallon. What the, almost life-size, polar bears (in front of Ruggins') are advertising isn't quite clear.

Church Corner, Hadleigh.

99 Hadleigh Church Bus Shelter
This card introduces the location of the southerly excursion. The road disappearing in the background is Castle Lane, leading to the Salvation Army Colony and the ruins of Hadleigh Castle.

CastleLane, Hadleigh.

100 Castle Lane, looking south
Circa 1900 these houses are probably amongst the first brick-built ones in the Lane (the corner of a wooden structure is visible opposite). They can just be seen in the card above and they all still exist in 2013, though the first (no. 36) has recently been extended and converted into flats.   *Ed. The last house in the row is in Beech Road (No. 56).*

Section 6.
Castle Lane to the Salvation Army Land and Industrial Colony started 1891

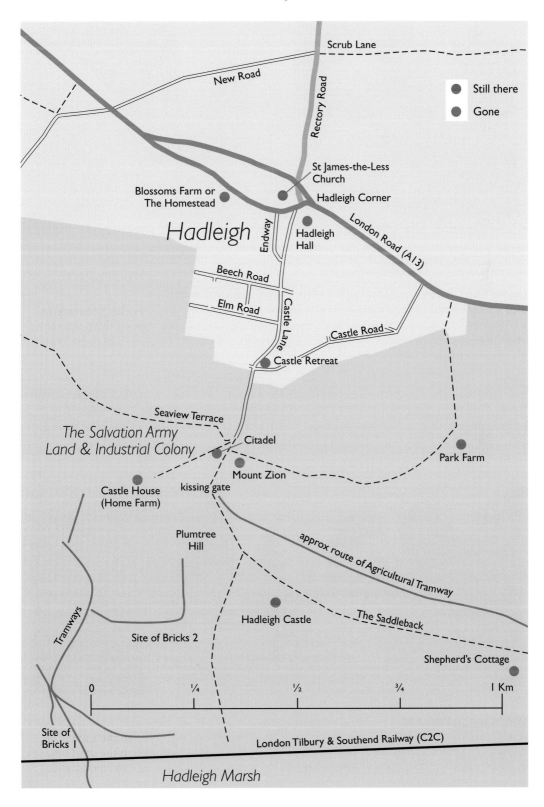

Scrub Lane

New Road

Rectory Road

● Still there

○ Gone

St James-the-Less Church

Blossoms Farm or The Homestead

Hadleigh Corner

London Road (A13)

Hadleigh

Endway

Hadleigh Hall

Beech Road

Elm Road

Castle Lane

Castle Road

Castle Retreat

Seaview Terrace

The Salvation Army Land & Industrial Colony

Citadel

Park Farm

Mount Zion

Castle House (Home Farm)

kissing gate

Plumtree Hill

approx route of Agricultural Tramway

The Saddleback

Tramways

Hadleigh Castle

Site of Bricks 2

Shepherd's Cottage

| 0 | ¼ | ½ | ¾ | 1 Km |

Site of Bricks 1

London Tilbury & Southend Railway (C2C)

Hadleigh Marsh

101 Castle Lane from junction with Castle Road, looking north

The writer of this card dates it 6-2-1929 and proves that shops are already plying for trade. The sun-blind reads E. Hyltons, luncheons and parties catered for. Also selling cigarettes and ices.

Ed. All these houses still exist (2013)

102 Shops in Castle Lane

A few years later E. Hylton is clearly doing well as two shops are visible, with that name on both as well as Castle Retreat. The farthest one has Confectioners painted over the windows and is purveying soft drinks and ices.

Castle Lane, Hadleigh.   112560

103 E. Hylton's Shop and Castle Retreat, 89 Castle Lane

The sign-board on the wall (over an older one) reads E. Hylton, Tea Rooms and Gardens, and over the side entrance the sign is Castle Retreat Tea Gardens. The distant buildings are those of the Salvation Army Farm Colony: the Dining Room, the School and Seaview Terrace.

Castle Retreat Tea Gardens (Side)   Hadleigh.   112590

104 Castle Retreat Tea Gardens

And here are the actual Tea Gardens with clean table-cloths and fresh flowers. Only one customer so far though, but the pot of tea is arriving – self-service was unheard of.

105 Castle Retreat Tea Gardens

This series of cards, (produced by Bells Photo Co Ltd of Leigh-on-Sea) was, presumably, commissioned by Hylton for marketing purposes and local sale only. Castle Road is just visible to the left.   *Ed. This card was sent by E. Hylton to the Reverend J. E. Bottoms of Southview, Ambleside Drive to advise him that his Sunday School outing was expected.*

106 The entrance to the Salvation Army Colony

This is the first of the two main destinations to which Castle Lane leads, The Salvation Army Land & Industrial Colony, founded 1891. At the gateway is the Home Superintendent's Office. The writer of this card postmarked 1909 makes no reference to the event being celebrated, but William Booth was 80 years old in April, 1909.

107 Salvation Army Land & Industrial Colony

The lane continues to the left, to Hadleigh Castle. Distinguished in his uniform, the postman with a bulging postbag (and a resplendent walrus moustache) is posing for the camera. Two of the colonists' dormitories are just visible down the lane to the left, between the trees. *Ed. This card is postmarked 1913.*

108 Salvation Army Home Farm (formerly Castle Farm)

It would appear to be a very early motorcycle that the cyclist is wheeling. But it is a later picture than the previous one: note the new wall built around the trees and the low barrier to prevent accidental falling down the steep incline. The Citadel is behind the Home Office and Castle House can be seen at the very end of Castle Avenue.

109 Castle House

As stated on the card this is Castle House (built 1706) so originally a farmhouse or even a manor house. Here *circa* 1900 it is the private dwelling of a senior Salvationist with two children. The man in the porch has goggles on his cap, so perhaps he was the motorcyclist in the last card?

110 Home Farm, Castle Avenue, looking west

This is the main street through the Farm Colony, but these buildings are all long gone, including the old farmhouse at the end. Nowadays, the Salvation Army Training Centre and Tea Rooms are situated on the left and the new farmhouse is in the centre.

111 Castle Avenue, looking east

Just what the flags and bunting are in aid of, is not clear, perhaps a visiting dignitary from London Headquarters? Note the water-fountain presented in 1901 by an American benefactor from New York.

Ed. The fountain was renovated in 2000 (except for the top piece, which had gone missing).

General View Salvation Army Colony, Hadleigh

112 A view towards Castle Avenue from the south-west

These must be the nursery slopes as a very young foal is lying close behind the mare, with the field to themselves. The building which looks like a shop (in line with the mare) is now the head office. The Citadel is on the right and the Boys' Dining Room is next to it.

CastleLane,Hadleigh.

113 Looking up Castle lane

This is the view up the hill from the gate in postcard 114. The top group are near to the Colony entrance, the nearer group, mainly children, have turned in order to display their bouquets to the photographer.
Ed. This card is postmarked 1909.

SALVATION ARMY COLONY, HADLEIGH. 41070.

114 A view of the Colony from the south

This family group are off to visit the castle at the end of this lane. The gate is normally locked to prevent traffic going there, the kissing gate allows entry for pedestrians. The large building in the centre is the Citadel, the place of worship, which was demolished in 2003.
Ed. This postcard is contemporary with cards 107 and 110.

Salvation Army Colony, Hadleigh.

115 Looking up Castle Lane from beneath the Castle

The kissing gate of the previous card is here seen from an elevated position, and also shows a length of the Castle approach road. A portion of the market garden is seen. *Ed. An agricultural tramway ran along this valley, towards Leigh. The Thundersley postmark is illegible but two halfpenny Edward VII stamps signifies after June 1918.*

Salvation Army Colony, Hadleigh

116 A view of the Colony from the Castle Mount

Through the trees (on the right side) two large houses are visible; this is Mount Zion, home to the Governor and S.A. officers. During the Great War soft fruits were grown in this area and my eldest brother was one of many school-children released to gather fruit. *Ed. The route of the tramway can be made out, along the valley.*

117 Hadleigh Castle

Here is seen the majority of the remains of Hadleigh Castle, built by Hubert De Burgh from 1215 onwards for the purpose of guarding the Thames Estuary from French invasion. It is viewed from close to the remains of the N.W. Tower looking in a south-easterly direction.

118 Remains of the north-west tower

The N.W. Tower viewed from the bailey. This castle was never involved in any defensive action and after passing through many occupiers, was finally sold off for salvage *circa* 1551 and extensively used for other buildings including, according to local folklore, St Clement's Church, Leigh-on-Sea.

119 Castle Sports Day
Prior to WW2, the Salvation Army used to organise a sports day or other attractions on Bank Holidays and this view, postmarked 1931, must be one of those occasions. Just what the man, the centre of attention, is about to do is not clear but in his elevated position he appears to be supporting a ladder. Is his intention to climb it?

120 Estuary View
Postmarked 1920, this view shows the remains of a once even more extensive marsh, the Thames Estuary and the creek which divides Canvey from Benfleet. Note the steam train en-route to Southend, and in particular the land slippage that has dragged down the remains of the south curtain wall. *Ed. Spot the shepherd's cottage, right of tower.*

HADLEIGH CASTLE . HADLEIGH . ESSEX .

121 The shepherd and his sheep

Whilst the S.E. Tower remains more or less in the same condition as in this view postmarked 1951, the N.E. one (on the left) has decayed further and is now just a pathetic spike. Note the shepherd and his dog, watching over this flock of ewes and their lambs (of which some thirty can be counted).

Hadleigh Castle.

122 Hadleigh Castle from the east, below the Saddleback

East of the towers, the undulations of the ground leave a considerable ridge known locally as the 'Saddleback' which gives a fine elevated view of the surrounding area for the initial section of a walk to Old Leigh.

123 Salvation Army Colony brickfields
Apart from its many varied agricultural training activities, the Salvation Army also had a thriving brick-making industry, at its peak having three brickfields. This view, postmarked 1929, is of the multiple kiln unit and stacks of finished bricks.

124 Brick kilns
It is not clear whether these wheelbarrow loads of bricks are for firing, or being removed for stacking, but their position could suggest the former. Each brick was identified as being produced by the Salvation Army Land Industrial Colony by the initials SALIC in the 'frog' i.e. the indentation in the top.

125 Clay quarry near Sayers Farm

Here the clay is seen being collected and part of the tramway system used for its transportation. A large pit like this one remained for several years, and the relative position of this one can be assessed by the silhouette of the Benfleet Water Tower in the distance.

126 Hard labour and redemption

Here, the clay is more readily accessible, needing two tram-line systems, and much has already been removed, by pick and shovel. Note that there is usually a uniformed overseer close by.

127 The hacks

The dictionary explains that 'hacks' were 'frames for drying bricks' but in this view most appear to be empty, so maybe they have all been dried as it appears to be a warm day. However the second and third hacks appear to contain bricks.

Ed. Note the wind pump – shortage of water was a perennial issue.

128 Brick-making

By 1893, just a couple of years after the Colony started, bricks were in mass production. Between 20 and 30 thousand could be produced in a day. Here eleven workers and the Overseer pose for the camera in front of some primitive and dangrous-looking machinery. Firing the clay made a terrible stench, hence the very tall chimneys on the kilns.

7. The growth of Hadleigh Corner and development of Transport

129 Hadleigh Hall

Hadleigh Hall was originally a grand private residence before becoming the property of the Salvation Army, who used it to house the Governor. In 1937 it was leased to Dr William James who, with Dr Samuel McGladdery, opened a surgery on the west side. The house was demolished in 1961 to make way for a row of shops and flats.

130 Hadleigh Colony Band

This is most probably a funeral procession but for many years the Salvation Army Band was a feature of village life, holding open-air Sunday morning services in various streets around the parish. The location is the head of the High Street, where the tea gardens had spread to the other side of the restaurant.

131 Hadleigh Corner

The final return to Hadleigh (or Church) Corner is used to show the increase in passenger services and facilities and also to commence the easterly route to Leigh and Southend-on-Sea.
Ed. The street-cleaner's handcart bears the legend E.C.C. and the signpost points south to the Salvation Army Citadel and east to the Fire Station (prior to its relocation in 1931).

132 The Triangle – waiting for the bus

By 1937 (as postmarked) the size of the triangle has increased considerably and even some seating and timetables are provided. The bus is destined for Leigh Station and the passengers' shadows indicate a mid-morning scene.
Ed. The Fire Station sign has been turned and the famous hexagonal seat has appeared.

The Corner, Hadleigh 38221

133 Hadleigh panorama 1

The destination board in the back window confirms that this bus (Reg. VX8014) is off to Benfleet, watched by the policeman. The Southend-bound bus (just visible) must have time to spare as the conductor is talking to the driver. *Ed. Note the Church vestry extension, built in 1928 by David Stibbards and designed by Sir Charles Nicholson.*

The Corner, Hadleigh. 138222

134 Hadleigh panorama 2

All westbound passengers have boarded either the new 'double-decker' (destination unknown), or the rear one which has Hadleigh and Tarpots on the destination board. *Ed. Yet another style of lamp post appears in the triangle but Daws Heath is still spelt the quaint way (Dawes). Possibly photographed the same day as card 133.*

The Triangle, Hadleigh.

135 The famous bus shelter at 'Hadleigh Church'
By 1938 (the date on this card) there is now a substantial 5-sided shelter provided around the hexagonal seat. The waiting bus is destined for Westleigh Schools, Leigh Church, Chalkwell Schools and Southend-on-Sea but no-one has boarded yet.

Hadleigh, Central Broadway.

FRITH
HLH 2

136 London Road, looking east from by the Church fence
And a little later the shelter has been glazed. More important, for this card, is the view down a busy London Road towards Southend.
Ed. The stripy-painted kerb may be relic from the War, to aid visibility in the 'blackout'.

Section 8.
The eastern route of the London Road towards Southend

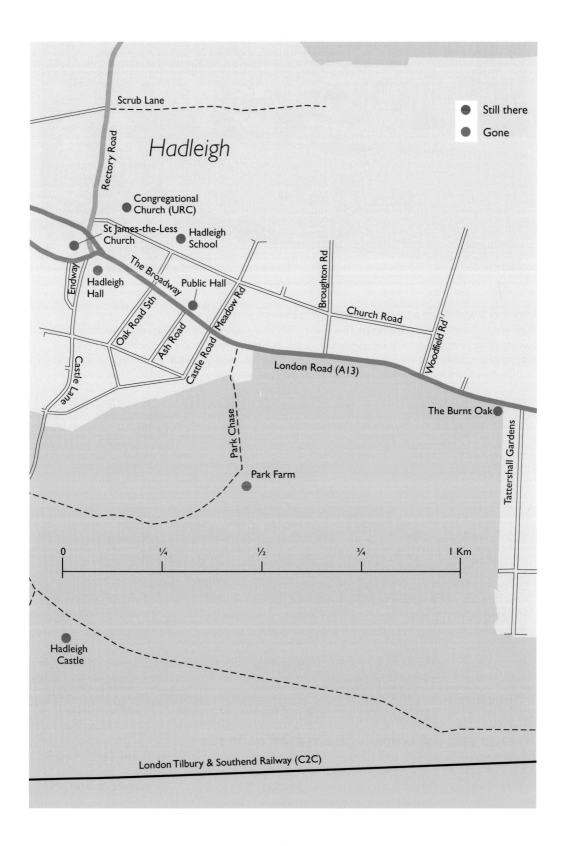

HADLEIGH, LONDON ROAD LOOKING EAST

137 London Road (also known as The Broadway), looking east

This premature card of the sequence *circa* 1947 is meant to give perspective to those which follow. The seated men are facing towards the triangle therefore it is a view of the north side of the London Road, east of the church. The hardware shop was owned by Mence Smith. Next is Ross the shoeshop and then Royce the barber. Note the L-plate on car.

138 House to shop conversions – London Road, north side

At the turn of the century, the four terraced houses seen on the previous card were isolated (although other groups existed further down the road) and the first shop to appear belonged to Mr Norman (possibly the originator). The garage on the corner of Rectory Road is the only other building in view, also Mr F. Norman's.

139 Approaching Hadleigh from the east, near Oak Road
Looking towards the church (hidden by trees) from a position close to Oak Road North, (not existing at this time) the rows of terraced housing spreads along the road. The block of houses in card 138 can just be seen plus the shop but this must be an earlier view as no kerbs appear here.

140 From still further east, near Ash Road area
Comparing the roads and kerbs in these two views, they must be of similar vintage. This one is taken further east from the south side of the road close to where Ash Road will occur. The shop proprietor is J. T. Jordison declaring himself as cornkeeper and dairy farmer. Note that there is no Oak Road exit visible.

141 London Road, north side

The wording on this sunblind is F. H. Norman & Co Garage, and motor spirit (not petrol) is available, either 'Pratts' or 'Carburine' also 'K S G Power' whatever that was – but no pumps are in view. The wooden hut appears to belong to a clock repairer, as a large round one is in the window. This card is postmarked September 1910.

142 London Road, Oak Road junction

This is a reverse view of the previous one but with two (at least) extra house/shop conversions. Oak Road North is that turning on the right leading to Hadleigh School and Church Road, with Oak Road South opposite. Where the houses are on the left, is now Lidl car park.

143 The Public Hall, London Road

A short distance further east of the viewpoint of card No. 140 is this *circa* 1930 one. The middle telegraph pole on the right side is the approximate position of the shop in that view. The tall building was known as The Public Hall, a very popular venue for a variety of social functions. Now it is a carpet sales emporium.

144 London Road, looking east

This post WWII view looking east reveals that all the house-fronts are now shops of one kind or another including Mence Smith, hardware; J. F. Ross, cobbler; W. S. Royce, hairdresser (who took over the establishment from Mr Emery) and Smith Read, bespoke tailor. Note the Albany Laundry van and the two passing buses in the distance.

145 Yes, we have some bananas!

Here at Owen Bros in the London Road, between Castle Road and Ash Road and dated 15th November 1945 is a queue of ladies (and children) desiring to savour the first bananas available since the end of WWII. Hopefully they all obtained generous bunches similar to those at the front of the queue. Owen's closed in Dec 1973 and the site has recently been redeveloped.

146 London Road, from junction with Castle Road, looking west in 1947

In 1947 or maybe a little before, from a position by Castle Road, the small café on the left precedes Page's newsagent, sweets & tobacco, then Owen Bros (seen in 145). On the other (north) side, at the corner of Meadow Road, is (No.4) J. W. Every, hardware; Gaskins, shoe repair service; a confectionery; Castle Cleaners and a bakery – all before the Public Hall.

APPROACHING HADLEIGH.

147 London Road, looking west *circa* **1930**

This very similar view to the preceding one, but *circa* 1930, exhibits a few differences i.e. removal contractors had the corner site. But the newsagent was already there and Owen's, who began business in Hadleigh in 1917. Opposite, S Clarke had the corner shop and E. F. Smith owned a butcher's shop in this block, whose delivery service is shown next.

148 Door-to-door delivery services

After WWII the area from Meadow Road to the Public Hall was taken over by Trevards children's clothing manufactory. Later it became Sketchley's dry cleaners and now Johnsons Apparelmasters (383 London Road). E. F. Smith traded from his butcher's shop in The Broadway (London Rd) from *circa* 1906 until *circa* 1914, prior to relocating to the High Street.

149 London Road, looking east from Castle Road

Circa 1917 Alice Smith was the proprietor of this shop at the junction of Castle Road and The Broadway (London Road) but, in the 1930s, it was Monk's the butcher. Next to them was Jackie Flatt's shop and yard: he had a big reputation for always being able to supply obsolete replacement parts when others could not, especially in the case of old wooden-roller mangles.

150 Beke Hall Farm Dairy. London Road

The previous card also shows C. Matthews's grocery store. This building was later extended to include others, of which E. W. Morton's dairy was one. This view can be closely dated, as the notice in the window reads 'Annual Flag Day Saturday 11ᵗʰ May 1935'.

Ed. It is unlikely that the driver would still be sporting his moustache in four years tme!

View Leigh Road, Hadleigh.   494.

151 London Road, looking east from Park Chase, *circa* 1916
The wall on the right is that seen in the distance on card 149 on the corner of Park Chase so this view of the London Road is from that position towards the eastern boundary marked by the Burnt Oak pillar where such a tree marked the boundary in the past. The big field on the right still affords, in 2013, one of the very finest views in the county.

View Leigh Road, Hadleigh.   493.

152 London Road towards Leigh, *circa* 1916
The conical roof of the first house seen here is just visible under the propping pole of the first telegraph pole in card 151 and so helps to position this view. Broughton Road will later be built just to the side of the second conical roofed property.

153 London Road, from junction with Broughton Road, looking east
Broughton Road just precedes Mansbridge & Watkin high class grocer's, which store, after some changes in ownership (including at one time the Post Office) is now part of Tower stores, selling domestic electrical appliances.

154 Huxtable's haberdashery, 'Hazelwood' 593 London Road
In card 153 between the two telegraph poles, a signboard and sun blind indicate this haberdashery run by two sisters, Rose and May Huxtable and here is a view of their shop windows. The price tags in shillings, equate to just pence in today's currency.
Ed. Nowadays, 593 London Road is a private dwelling.

155 Congregational Church, Church Road

Hadleigh Congregational Church was built close to the west end of Church Road. The sign reads Sunday School but with so many adults, Boys' Brigade members and Union flags, a rather more important occasion is indicated. It is still in much the same condition but now known as Hadleigh United Reformed Church.

156 Hadleigh School, Church Road, built 1910

Here is Hadleigh Council School, built in Church Road opposite Oak Road North, in 1910. Access must have been difficult over so much mud, but a hard surface was constructed to just past the corner of the railings until the road was made up *circa* 1930. It is now the Junior School. *Ed. Plans are afoot to build a new school nearby and develop this site for housing.*

157 Poors Lane

Some of the remnants of the once extensive forests in and around Hadleigh remain after much depletion in the past for ship building purposes. This view is, as I remember, Poors Lane *circa* 1930 leading from Daws Heath Road to Bramble Hall and the northern access to Belfairs Wood.

158 The Woods, off Scrub Lane, *circa* 1911

'The Woods' was a cul-de-sac into the woods off Scrub Lane, which led from Rectory Road (opposite New Road) to Belfairs Woods and the golf course. These two (of three) houses still exist – though much altered – and a few modern ones have been added.

159 The Great War
To conclude this brief history in postcards of early 1900s Hadleigh and Thundersley and
to remember its participation in World War 1, here is a parade through the High Street
(past Mr Emery's hairdressing facility and the village policeman).

160 Lest we forget
And this is a card printed for soldiers as a souvenir of their stay or visit.

1902-1904
(Edward VII)

1904-1910
(Edward VII)

51911-1912
(George V)

1912-1918
(George V)

1918-1921
(George V)

A brief history of postcards in Britain and clues to identifying their age

Postcards were first introduced in Britain by the Post Office in 1870. These early postcards bore an embossed ½d stamp and were thinner and smaller than the present-day type. the address appeared one side and the message on the other. No charge was made by the Post Office for the postcard itself.

In 1894, after much lobbying from stationers, permission was granted for the use of commercially produced postcards to which a halfpenny adhesive stamp could be fixed. The age of the Picture Postcard had begun.

From 1899 onwards, the standard size (already in use in other countries) of 3½" by 5½" was accepted in Britain.

However, only the address, and nothing else, could be written on the front of the card. The message went on the back, often sharing the space with a picture.

In 1902 the Post Office led the field, changing its rules to allow a division on the address side, so that the left-hand side could be used for a message. Often a line was printed to mark the division.

A legible postmark clearly establishes the latest possible date of a postcard's production but, of course, the card might have been published many years earlier (or, indeed, the photograph could be from an even earlier date. If the date is not legible, the stamp can be a guide.

The normal (inland) postage rate for postcards remained at ½d for almost 50 years, until 1918.

On 3rd June 1918 the inland rate was doubled to 1d, resulting in a decline in the number of postcards posted. Within three years there was a further increase to 1½d. However, in the wake of much ill-feeling, during May 1922 it was reduced back to a penny.

In 1925 new international sizes for postcards were adopted, being Maximum 5⅞" x 4⅛" Minimum 4" x 2¾"

In May 1940 the postcard rate rose to 2d. There were to be two further increases, to 2½d in 1957 and 3d in 1965, before the Special Rate for Postcards was finally abolished in May 1965.

Postcards can also be roughly dated by the portrait on the stamp. This is not *quite* as easy as it sounds because the sovereign's name does not feature – and both Edward VII (1901–1910) and George V (1910–1936) appear balding and bearded!

In the days before widespread ownership of telephones, postcards were, in effect, 'the poor man's telegram'. Three deliveries a day meant that a sailor could arrive in port early morning and, quite literally, write to his wife that she might expect him home for tea that same day.

Picture postcards were sometimes collected as keepsakes, but more on account of their pictures than their messages: yet few of our ancestors would have imagined that these humble items of ephemera would hold us quite so spell-bound a century later!

© David Hurrell

1921-1922
George V)

| 1922-1934 (George V) | 1934-1936 (George V) | 1937-1940 (George VI) | 1940-1952 (George VI) |